Lire à petits pas Niveau

Méthode Montessori pour apprendre à lire : du mot au livre

French English German Spanish - Afrikaans

hoe

houe

houe

azada

hoe

Use a hoe in the garden.

way

façon

façon

camino

manier

They find a way back home.

leg

jambe

jambe

pierna

been

My leg is feeling better.

face   visage

visage

cara   gesig

They were at the face painting booth.

---

boy   garçon

garçon

chico   seuntjie

The boy is eating dinner.

---

bird   oiseau

oiseau

pájaro   voël

The bird is dancing happily.

watch   l'horloge

l'horloge

reloj   Watch

My watch is ticking.

---

man   homme

homme

hombre   man

This man is my dad.

---

rain   pluie

pluie

lluvia   reën

We love the rain!

conditions   conditions

conditions

condiciones   voorwaardes

What are the weather conditions.

---

morning   matin

Matin

mañana   oggend

I wake up in the morning.

---

dog   chien

chien

perro   hond

The dog wants to eat sweets.

| day | journée |
| día | dag |

journée

This day is the 30th.

| oxygen | oxygène |
| oxígeno | suurstof |

oxygène

What is the symbol for oxygen?

| squirrel | écureuil |
| ardilla | eekhoring |

écureuil

The squirrel is on the tree.

bed

lit

lit

cama

bed

We all share three beds.

---

corn

blé

blé

maíz

koring

I grow corn in the garden.

---

hill

colline

colline

colina

Hill

The house is on the hill.

stick   bâton

bâton

palo   stok

He is playing sticks.

---

fresh   frais

Frais

fresco   vars

All the fruit is fresh.

---

tree   arbre

arbre

árbol   boom

She is sitting under a tree.

Hommes

The men are arguing.

sœur

She is my sister.

temps

He is telling the time.

eye

œil

œil

ojo

oog

He is closing his eyes.

letter

alphabet

alphabet

alfabeto

alfabet

Learn English letters is fun.

father

père

père

papá

pa

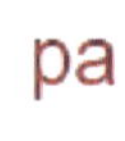

He is a nice father.

duck   canard

canard

pato   eend

The duck is swimming.

---

school   école

école

colegio   skool

They are going to school.

---

food   aliments

aliments

comida   kos

They made a lot of food.

church
église

église

iglesia
kerk

Did you go to church?

name
nom

Nom

nombre
naam

My name is Joe.

brother
frère

frère

hermano
broer

They are brothers.

family | famille

famille

familia | gesin

How big is your family?

---

place | endroit

endroit

sitio | plek

This is my favorite place.

---

seed | la graine

la graine

semilla | saad

We will plant the seeds.

cat   chat

chat

gato   kat

That cat is adorable.

France   france

France

francia   Frankryk

Have you ever been to France?

baby   bébé

bébé

bebé   baba

The baby is crawling.

sun | soleil

Soleil

dom | son

The sun is very bright.

---

milk | lait

Lait

leche | melk

The baby is drinking milk.

---

example | exemple

exemple

ejemplo | byvoorbeeld

This is an example of a bird.

score

but

But

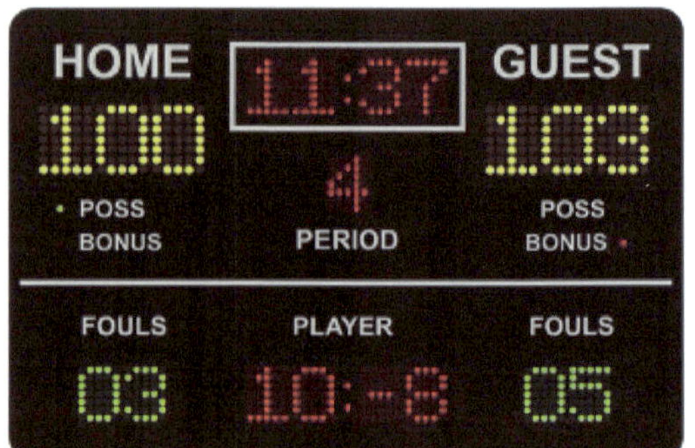

puntuación

telling

What was the final score?

---

fire

feu

Feu

fuego

vuur

Fire is hot.

---

paper

papier

papier

papel

papier

I like to color on paper.

door   porte

porte

puerta   deur

He is knocking on the door.

city   ville

ville

cludad   Stad

He worked in the city.

four   quatre

quatre

cuatro   vier

There were four of them.

robin robin

Robin

robin robin

The robin is helping Santa.

---

game jeu

Jeu

juegos spel

What game is it?

---

children les enfants

les enfants

niños kinders

Four children sang.

ground

sol

sol

suelo

grond

It plays a trick on the ground.

---

farm

ferme

ferme

granja

plaas

The farm has lots of animals.

---

thing

chose

chose

cosa

ding

I am thinking of many things.

company compagnie

compagnie

empresa   maatskappy

What company do you work for?

---

nest   nid

nid

nido   nes

The bird has a nest.

---

flower   fleur

fleur

flor   blom

She is holding a flower.

table

table

table

mesa

tafel

There is a toy on the table.

seat

siège

siège

aslento

sitplek

The girls took a seat in the sand.

doll

poupée

poupée

muñeca

Pop

She is hugging her doll.

goodbye   au revoir

Au revoir

adiós   totsiens

The bear is saying goodbye.

---

page   page

page

página   bladsy

Please turn the page.

---

birthday   anniversaire

anniversaire

cumpleaños   verjaarsdag

Today is my birthday.

mother   mère

mère

madre   moeder

My mother loves me.

fish   poisson

poisson

pez   vis

There are two fish.

grass   herbe

herbe

césped   gras

The goat is eating the grass.

farmer

fermier

fermier

agricultor

boer

The farmer had a farm.

---

feet

pieds

pieds

pies

voete

His feet are swollen.

---

horse

cheval

cheval

caballo

perd

The horse is galloping.

bread   pain

pain

un pan   brood

She is baking some bread.

---

kitty   minou

minou

gatlto   kitty

I like my kitty.

---

street   rue

rue

calle   straat

They walk across the street.

nose   nez

nez

nariz   neus

My nose is running.

---

money   argent

argent

dinero   geld

I save money in my piggy bank.

---

coat   manteau

manteau

saco   Jas

She is wearing her coat.

apple   pomme

Pomme

manzana   appel

Apples are a popular fruit.

---

egg   oeuf

Oeuf

huevo   eier

The bunny has many eggs.

---

floor   sol

sol

suelo   vloer

The girl sits on the floor.

wood   bois

bois

madera   hout

He plays with wooden blocks

---

chart   graphique

graphique

gráfico   grafiek

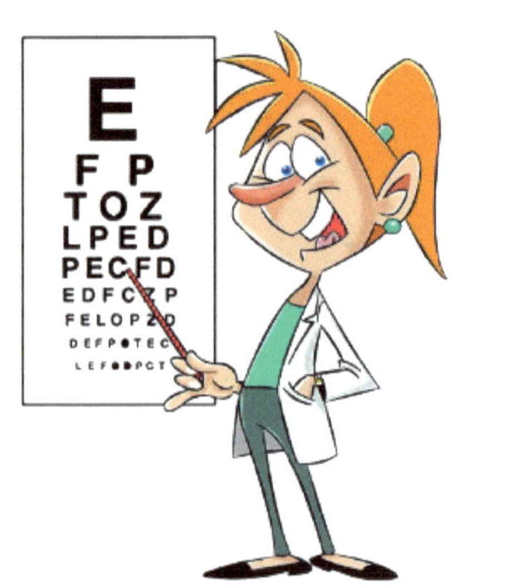

What does your medical chart say?

---

boat   bateau

bateau

barco   boot

The boat is sailing.

water

l'eau

l'eau

agua

water

He is drinking water.

---

toy

jouet

jouet

juguete

speelding

He has a whole box of toys.

---

cow

vache

vache

vaca

koei

The cow is standing up.

hand   main

main

mano   hand

You should wash your hands.

rabbit   lapin

lapin

conejo   haas

The rabbit wants to play.

chair   chaises

chaises

sillas   stoel

He is sitting on the chair.

pig   porc

porc

cerdo   vark

She is lying on the pig.

girl   fille

fille

niña   meisie

The girl is pretty.

house   maison

maison

casa   huis

We live in the same house.

snow

neige

neige

nieve

sneeu

I have fun in the snow.

idea

idée

idée

idea

idee

I have an idea!

rose

rose

Rose

rosa

roos

Thank you for the rose.

rope   corde

corde

cuerda   tou

Do you have any rope?

ball   balle

Balle

pelota   bal

He is bouncing the ball.

sheep   mouton

mouton

oveja   skape

The sheep have fluffy wool.

home   maison

maison

casa   huis

He drew a picture of his home.

---

bell   cloche

cloche

campana   klok

I hear the bell ringing!

---

night   nuit

nuit

noche   nag

We sleep at night.

gun

pistolet

pistolet

pistola

gewere

We played with a water gun.

---

children

les enfants

les enfants

niños

kinders

The children are playing.

---

wind

vent

vent

viento

wind

The wind blows the leaves.

Greek   grec

grec

griego   Griekse

Have you ever had Greek food?

---

window   fenêtre

fenêtre

ventana   venster

The window is open.

---

cotton   coton

coton

algodón   katoen

A q-tip is made of cotton.

shoe　　　　　　　　chaussure

chaussure

zapato　　　　　　　skoen

I have new shoes.

---

column　　　　　　　colonne

colonne

columna　　　　　　kolom

Did you read the newspaper column?

---

garden　　　　　　　jardin

jardin

jardín　　　　　　　tuin

They are going to the garden.

top

haut

Haut

tapas

tops

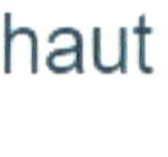

We like to play with tops.

---

box

boîte

boîte

caja

boks

The box is full of clothes.

---

song

chanson

chanson

canciones

lied

She is singing a song.

ring   bague

bague

anillo   ring

The bird is holding a ring.

picture   image

image

imagen   prent

He is taking some pictures.

chicken   poulet

poulet

pollo   hoender

The chicken is laying eggs.

party

fête

fête

fiesta

partytjie

I love to go to parties.

---

car

voiture

voiture

coche

voertuig

My car is fast

---

bear

ours

ours

oso

beer

The bear likes to eat honey.

office   bureau

Bureau

oficina   kantoor

Do you need any office supplies?

---

head   tête

tête

cabeza   kop

She has a hat on her head.

---

cake   gâteau

gâteau

pastel   koek

The cake is white and pink.

www.ingramcontent.com/pod-product-compliance
Lightning Source LLC
Chambersburg PA
CBHW041645110726
48005CB00003B/713